CHASING GRATITUDE

A JOURNEY OF RECOVERY IN FREE VERSE

By Douglas R. Boyer

TEACH Services, Inc.
PUBLISHING
www.TEACHServices.com • (800) 367-1844

World rights reserved. This book or any portion thereof may not be copied or reproduced in any form or manner whatever, except as provided by law, without the written permission of the publisher, except by a reviewer who may quote brief passages in a review.

The author assumes full responsibility for the accuracy of all facts and quotations as cited in this book. The opinions expressed in this book are the author's personal views and interpretations, and do not necessarily reflect those of the publisher.

This book is provided with the understanding that the publisher is not engaged in giving spiritual, legal, medical, or other professional advice. If authoritative advice is needed, the reader should seek the counsel of a competent professional.

Copyright © 2023 Douglas R. Boyer
Copyright © 2023 TEACH Services, Inc.
ISBN-13: 978-1-4796-0616-0 (Paperback)
ISBN-13: 978-1-4796-0617-7 (ePub)
Library of Congress Control Number: 2022923372

Unless otherwise indicated, all Scripture quotations are taken from the King James Version (KJV) of the Bible. Public domain.

Scripture quotations marked (NLT) are taken from the Holy Bible, New Living Translation, copyright © 1996, 2004, 2007 by Tyndale House Foundation. Used by permission of Tyndale House Publishers, Inc., Carol Stream, Illinois 60188. All rights reserved.

Scripture quotations marked (NKJV) are taken from the New King James Version®. Copyright © 1982 by Thomas Nelson, Inc. Used by permission. All rights reserved.

www.TEACHServices.com • (800) 367-1844

ACKNOWLEDGEMENT

I want to thank the staff at TEACH Services, Inc. for believing in this project, their support and words of encouragement. Also, I want to thank the many who contributed donations to help bring this work into the light. May the Lord's blessing rain upon your life, keeping you in your walk with Him. Giving honor to the Father, I want to thank God for entrusting in me, the inspiration to write this book. The many tears I have cried while doing His work, reflect the growth, humility and trust He has planted in me.

I thank you all.

TABLE OF CONTENTS

Acknowledgement   iii
Foreword   vii
I Love You All   ix
For Tracey   xi
From the Author   xiii

Part 1. The Loner's Anthem   17

Introductory Essay: Hope for the Sinner   19
From the Author: Sin Separates   20
DAY 1.   False Freedom   20
DAY 2.   Ribbon of Smoke   24
DAY 3.   Welcome Home   27
DAY 4.   Anxious   32
DAY 5.   Broken   36
DAY 6.   Self-Destruction   40
DAY 7.   The Door   44
DAY 8.   Greed   49
DAY 9.   Desire   54
DAY 10. Conflicted   58

Part 2. Spiritual Awakening 63

Introductory Essay: Incarcerated Freedom, a Prison State of Mind 65

From the Author: Jail House Poems 67

DAY 11. Half Shady 68

DAY 12. Prophetic Dream 72

DAY 13. The Prisoner 76

DAY 14. Sentenced 81

DAY 15. Society's One Vest 85

DAY 16. Lines of Insanity 89

DAY 17. Infectious Beauty 94

DAY 18. Forgive Me 98

DAY 19. Real Men 102

DAY 20. Chasing Gratitude 107

Part 3. Life after Death 111

Introductory Essay: Wow—What a Journey! 113

From the Author: The Journey 115

DAY 21. Day Dream 116

DAY 22. Why? 120

DAY 23. Victorious 125

DAY 24. Solutions 130

DAY 25. Daniel 4 134

DAY 26. My Steps 138

DAY 27. Dark Paths 142

DAY 28. Deceived 147

DAY 29. Darkness to Redemption 152

DAY 30. A Sinner's Prayer 157

Memorial

FOREWORD

Chasing Gratitude is the recounting of a journey driven by the Spirit of God and gratitude. Each successive part builds on the previous. It can be an awakening experience for all readers, no matter what their challenges in life. The insightful reflections help the partaker to relive and evaluate choices. Everyone who struggles with the enslaving power of sin can relate.

This book can be used as a daily devotional. With prayerful surrender to the leading of the Spirit, it can and will help a person meet the mission of 1 Peter 1:13–16:

> Wherefore gird up the loins of your mind, be sober, and hope to the end for the grace that is to be brought unto you at the revelation of Jesus Christ; as obedient children, not fashioning yourselves according to the former lusts in your ignorance: but as he which hath called you is holy, so be ye holy in all manner of conversation; because it is written, Be ye holy; for I am holy.

Readers who prayerfully read the poems and scriptures and then answer the accompanying thought questions can expect growth and enrichment.

It is with deep appreciation for the work of Douglas R. Boyer that I recommend his inspiring book. May the blessings of God be showered on you, the reader, partake.

Ezra Mendinghall
Pastor Northeast SDA Church, Charlotte, North Carolina
Master of Divinity, Andrews Theological Seminary
Bachelors of Arts, Oakwood University

I LOVE YOU ALL

To my family:
I want to apologize and thank you for not giving up on me. It would have been easy for you to walk away. In this day and time, that seems to be the way out for many. Though you were not happy and often distanced yourselves from me, you have chosen to stay a part of my life. For that, I am truly grateful and humbled.

To my children—Tiffany, Brittney, and Michael:
You endured the good, the worst, and the ugly up close. I love you dearly. Please forgive me. Know that your prayers have been answered, and our family can and will now survive, with the Lord's blessings, for He is truly with us. Mom Shirley, you have prayed many years for a healthy, happy son. Your prayers have not gone unanswered. The Lord your God is still in the prayer-answering business.

To my extended family:
Ms. T. Gray and her son Ray, thank you for answering God's call to serve. Disciples of Christ Ministries at the Northeast Seventh-day Adventist Church, Charlotte, North Carolina, I am grateful that you opened my eyes to my true calling, expanding my knowledge, my faith, and my trust in the Lord. Northeast Seventh-day Adventist Church family, thank you for your love and support along my journey. Pastor Ezra

Mendinghall, under your guidance, the call to service has become an important component of my life and message.

To my beautiful wife Tracey:
I have always said that God placed you in my life to save my life. You are my angel, and I am blessed each day because of you. To you, I present the following poem:

FOR TRACEY

Complex essence of femininity you are
Reaching for stars guided by moonlight.
My love struggles to understand
What you have found in this complex man.

You've turned my darkness into day
The rose glasses you once wore, stripped away.
A new reality gives life and love
As we together discover our way.

Pain and heartache we both endure
In life and the house of the Lord.
Perseverance proves, with faith, He can cure.
The enemy pulled but God restored.

This life has many a trail.
In God we must trust, or we will fail.
Hold to me, as I hold to you
As God's love guides us through.

May His blessings continue to shower upon our lives as we grow old together.

FROM THE AUTHOR

When I rewind and review the tape of my life, what is most astonishing is that I survived all the mistakes that I have made. Job captured our dependence on God and puzzlement over the trials that He allows in: "Although you know I am not guilty, no one can rescue me from your hands. You formed me with your hands; you made me, yet now you completely destroy me" (Job 10:7, 8, NLT).

Choice is our most fundamental freedom and the basis of the great controversy, which is the struggle between good and evil. Making good choices is what sermons, gospel teaching, and church programs attempt to teach. My life has been a series of lessons, sometimes like the coupling of cars in a train switchyard. In the switchyard, cars of different types are joined together, sent from different places according to a master plan. Once together, the different cars become a train.

Much of human experience does not always seem so orderly. A large share of my life has been more like the falling of dominoes, with one sinful and worldly act knocking over another. Unlike the switchyard, where cars smoothly link for a useful purpose, falling dominos crash into one another. In my life, one self-destructive episode has collided with the next, leaving one stage after another from which to recover before figuring out where I am and moving on.

Chasing Gratitude is a biography of different periods in my life. (Each period has an introductory essay in this book.) The world may seem like a very dark place when seen through my eyes. For many years, it was just that in many ways. I struggled with insecurity and uncertainty for most of my life, all the while smiling for the camera as people looked on. In many of the poems, I use the word "death" in a figurative sense. Sometimes it represents darkness and trouble; other times, it represents spiritual or physical pain. Ultimately, it was feeling "death" that led me to recognize my need of help. Jesus promised: "I will never leave you, nor forsake you." He has kept that promise, even when I mentally and physically left Him.

Thank God for Calvary! Thank God for the gift of salvation!

Douglas Boyer

Part 1
The Loner's Anthem

HOPE FOR THE SINNER

The command of God for us to be holy, I believe, lies outside the human sphere. We are born into sin and evil, yet God expects us to be holy as He is. This means having abhorrence towards sin as God does. It means that no sin or defilement can exist within His presence. It puzzles the human soul that we are not consumed when we, as sinners, come before God to pray and worship. The standards of conduct we find in God's holy Ten Commandments are holiness, righteousness, and integrity. The life that the first pair lived in the Garden of Eden was holy unto God. In their righteousness, they were without blemish or taint of sin. Through disobedience, their integrity was introduced to sin. Sin, an intruder that merits the wages of death, came into God's perfect universe. Nonetheless, there is hope in God by putting on the divine nature of Christ.

Peter calls upon us to gird up the loins of our mind. Our mind is to be subjected to the mind of Christ. The mind needs to be protected, kept sound, and empowered to resist sin and evil by the working of the Holy Spirit. The intoxication of sin—that is, the lust of the eyes, the lust of the flesh, and the pride of life—must not be allowed to consume us. Falling out of God's way, we become misguided and subject to the devil's ownership and control of our lives.

As Brother Douglas wrote in "Self-Destruction" (the poem for "Day 6"): "God watches the horror, and He lets it be." Why does God do this? It is because it is the road that we have chosen in spite of His calling us to travel the good way. God's Spirit says: "This is the way, walk ye in it" (Isaiah 30:21). When we neglect the voice of God in our life, it is inevitable that we will stray from the way of life into the way of death.

The wise man Solomon said, "For a just man falleth seven times, and riseth up again: but the wicked shall fall into mischief" (Prov. 24:16). This proverb is not a license to sin; it is an encouragement to do justly and walk humbly before God. God helps us to rise up and live holy before Him and not fall back into evil. The Christian is called to absolute holy living in Christ Jesus, living without sin.

Samuel Ryan
Elder Northeast SDA Church, Charlotte, North Carolina
Master of Divinity, Andrews University
Masters Education Brooklyn College

SIN SEPARATES

Sin and selfishness dominate the spirit of humankind and are the fundamental flaws in our character. They did not originate with God, for He designed humans to live unselfishly, which we can do under the power of the Holy Spirit. Nonetheless, when our base selfishness is expressed, life becomes toxic.

God has a spiritual design for humanity. Yet, humanity has decided that we can do what we want, when we want, where we want, and the way we want. Our minuscule sense of self stands in defiance of God. However, when we surrender our will to God and trust in Him, life and its struggles become simple, and gratitude becomes our motivation.

The heavenly Father designed us to love and serve others, for love is more powerful than the selfishness that drives society. Unhealthy lifestyles and environments of our own choosing cause us to miss opportunities for sharing and companionship; instead we selfishly go our own lonely way.

The loner's anthem is to be left alone. Yet, the loner is incapable of sharing ideas or even conversation with others. He misses the enjoyment of the wholesome social side of life. However, this can be turned around if he develops relationships, beginning with a relationship with God the Father. Though God lives in heaven above, we can develop a relationship with Him, and that positive relationship will affect the loner's human relationships, which he or she has been avoiding.

Day 1.

FALSE FREEDOM

Life extended through a tube,
Missing hours spent in solitude.
A dark hole illuminated by a flicker.
A dead zone, a death, with few exemptions.

The loneliness, please be quiet!
My spirit churns within the solace.
Life outside my hollow door dies.
God's grace slips away before my eyes.

Drip, drip, saline fills my veins.
The sword of righteousness calls my name.
This freedom locks my brain.
I seek Your mercy though I'm stained.

Confused, I play the game again.
Death calls for freedom; righteousness is vain.
Within four corners, a coliseum of shame,
False freedom, the price paid to make a name.

False Freedom

A healing star arises in the night.
Man has stolen the bride of Christ.
My soul is flushed with mercy's truth.
Death, not freedom, reigns in the tube.

Reflection

Life for many consists in things. It is not unusual for people to look to their possessions to find their worth, even though material things will not last forever. It is also common for people to find a sense of freedom through alcohol and drug uses. Both controlled me. For many years, my life revolved around addiction. I was a functioning addict, holding onto the false enjoyment of my unhealthy lifestyle. It was fun at first—until the newness wore off. Then the pleasure I got began to diminish by the year, then by the month, and finally by the day. In the end, my "freedom" under addiction became a living nightmare.

My story is not unique. Many have suffered under the taskmaster of addiction. Many are infatuated by the lure of material things, whether it is cars, clothes, money, or something else. Things become our focus and our addiction. Addiction controlled my life until faith in something greater than myself redirected my energies. I am grateful to know, today that I have a Father in heaven who never gave up on me.

Prayer

Heavenly Father, grabbing the reins of my life to go contrary to Your will left me lonely and cold. Please forgive me, and take the reins, guiding me in all Your ways.

Thought

Regardless of what you believe about organized religion or the one named Jesus, know this: Jesus came to take away the stain of your sins. If you have not made a profession of Him, all you need to do is acknowledge that Jesus came to live on earth, died on the cross for your sins, and rose again, thereby defeating death.

Scripture

"How long, O you sons of men, Will you turn my glory to shame? How long will you love worthlessness and seek falsehood?" (Psalm 4:2, NKJV)

Group/Individual Study

A. Begin with prayer.
B. Read the scripture.
C. Reflect on the scripture.
D. Answer the thought questions.

Thought Questions

1. What indulgence of yours is a dead zone?

2. How does a person get right with God? Is righteousness guaranteed to every Christian?

3. Daniel survived the lion's den through faith. In all honesty, where do you place your faith?

4. Is your faith killing you, or is it giving you life?

Day 2.

RIBBON'S OF SMOKE

Ribbons of white smoke make me take flight,
Traveling to places offering new heights.
I stagger, I fail, not in His rest.
Higher than a kite, but a step from death.

Deprivation holds the hunger fast.
My scourge flows in ribbons past.
A craving, I shriek notwithstanding
In a flash, it goes twice as fast.

Have I arrived, at my new address?
Voices of death know what is best.
On point and craftiness gains respect.
Ribbons calm, recognize you are whacked.

Your life fizzled—it did not die.
It went up in smoke out like light.
Reboot, redefine the ribbon that you rode.
Choose ribbons of life not those of smoke.

Ribbon's of Smoke

Reflection

When I was young, I smoked marijuana like so many of my peers. I followed the crowd, desperately seeking their acceptance. This was Satan's trap for me, and I do not make this admission lightly.

Marijuana allowed me to be like those I thought that I admired, and it allowed me to have something that they had, which I lacked—confidence. Along the way, I mastered the art of "fast talk" to meet girls. As my life changed, I believed I had arrived.

Satan's trap was wide open, and I fell into a deep hole. My life became a break-neck roller coaster ride of highs, lows, and sharp curves. Looking back, I see that I lost so much. I lost time, opportunities, memories, and, most of all, quality of life. The "good times" were nothing more than skewed memories, which I often embellished in telling others about them. Because I lost so many memories, I can only remember the so-called good times. The bad times—my destructive behavior and craziness—are, at best, but flashes that come and go.

Prayer

Christ, please let me be a beacon so that I may draw lost souls to You, offering my voice to deter others from falling into traps of Satan's designing.

Thought

I reached "new heights," but it was only short-term joy. I believe that is all Satan has to offer—short-term gratification. My preference now has changed to long-term salvation.

Scripture

"Then he looked toward Sodom and Gomorrah, and toward all the land of the plain; and he saw, and, behold, the smoke of the land which went up like the smoke of a furnace." (Gen. 19:28, NKJV)

Group/Individual Study

A. Begin with prayer.
B. Read the scripture.
C. Reflect on the scripture.
D. Answer the thought questions.

Thought Questions

1. Deprivation results in a reduction of benefits. What do we lose when we reject God?

2. Can we truly find rest in the Word of God?

3. Religious institutions and some lay people believe that they are the authority responsible for interpreting the Word of God. Should we rely solely upon their teaching? Why?

4. What does the Bible say about what matters most?

Day 3.

WELCOME HOME

Running towards that impulse called death.
It is seductive and cunning, the fun that He is not
The solitary time welcomes his control.
I push back, but death is too strong.

Running toward that impulse called death.
It greets me with open arms.
As the fat lady sings, it sings and flees, laughing at me.
Such an addictive pain that I enjoy again and again.

Sorrow knows no bounds, just grief.
The grief that welcomes me home each time I leave,
Hiding my life from help offers sincere.
The fear and shame the memorable rejections of my youthful years.

Laughs and jeers that I still hear follow me through the latter years.
Yet, I can't let them go, the bond is great, the connection that makes me.
Death, you see, follows me with open arms, welcoming me each time I leave.

Belief in something greater than me, aids the pain, the struggles remain.

The cross He was forced to wear to death's place, the burden I see.
They were belligerent to Him like others to me.
He loved, yet they laughed and jeered Him to death's place, you see.
So then, who am I that He would set me free? Death, you see.

He gave His life wearing that cross. After three days, death fled, and I was set free.
The past still haunts me, though it need not be.
For His blood was shed for me to cleanse the stains of rejection.
It is I who holds them dear, for I fear losing that part of me.
Therefore, I run back to death each time I depart.

Reflection
The lies we tell ourselves in pursuit of our fleshly desires are usually destructive and egocentric. We achieve what we seek only to discover it is not what we imagined. Then fantasy tells us that we must have done something wrong, because someone else we know is happy pursuing fleshly desires. Thus, we do them again and again achieving the same result. The definition of insanity is repeating the same behavior and expecting different results.

This is what my life was like for many years. I believed that I was doing it all wrong and, if I could only do it like "so-and-so," I would be happy. The truth is that so-and-so's life was in total ruins. However, because so-and-so projected the illusion of happiness, I wanted what I saw. How naïve can a guy be!

I didn't have this insight back then, so I continued seeking things that were imaginary and unsustainable. By the choices we make, we put ourselves on a predestined path in life. Some of us are blessed along the way to change course and achieve our dreams. Others of us achieve our dreams without understanding what we have accomplished. Therefore, we do not appreciate our achievement. When I had the opportunity to reflect on what I had accomplished, I cried. The death of the "old man" meant for me a new life with new opportunities. The greatest of these would be the opportunity to keep God continually before me.

Prayer
Lord God, You give knowledge to those who seek it. Please grant me wisdom to follow Your loving design for me and not the egocentric path of covetousness.

Thought
I knew it wasn't good for me, but I chased it again and again. Covetousness is chasing someone else's dream. When do we

ever learn? *Do we* ever learn? Or, is repetition a part of growth no matter where it takes us?

Scripture
"Is Israel a servant? Is he a homeborn slave? Why is he plundered?" (Jer. 2:14, NKJV)

Group/Individual Study

A. Begin with prayer.
B. Read the scripture.
C. Reflect on the scripture.
D. Answer the thought questions.

Thought Questions

1. What are you chasing—life or death?

2. How do you learn? Is open-mindedness and a willing heart all that is needed to obtain salvation?

3. Does the sight of a crucifix cause you to think about Jesus' sacrifice? Why?

4. Ask yourself: Is chasing that thing really greater than my soul's salvation?

Day 4.

ANXIOUS

Who am I? I am fear—the pain you've traveled with for years,
The anxiety you hold onto.
The pain that devours the willing, the scared
I am your battle and all your cares that block escape.

The will that denies your freedom
I am awed by your strength.
Awe, breathe me, birth me, live for me, all
Praying for freedom you run from it.

Desire to be rescued reject it, it is okay
Feel the roiling waves and reverence me; I am your disease.
Examine your weaknesses, weak joints and shallow brakes
Broken years of neglect, reach for an anointment

God is the strength that lives to release your torment
Show zeal for the Word, for faith is a gift.
Fear is not your healing; congregate, praise, and worship
The inheritance clears, when faith comes without fear.

Reflection
Through much of my formal years, I feared hearing laughter and jeering comments, even when they were not directed at me. My self-esteem was so low that these gestures triggered an inferiority complex. So, I would hide myself in academics and on the field of sports—whether it was baseball, basketball, or football. In these arenas, I really shined. In these I had no self-esteem problems.

However, what I felt inside haunted me for years. As I got older, I was uncomfortable being around people, constantly feeling that I did not belong. Eventually, I found a kind of employment in which I could work alone. Excelling in that environment, I was left all alone. Isolating myself from the world around me opened the door to selfishness, personal pride, and arrogance.

At the bottom of this spiral, I crashed. Today, I thank my Lord and Savior, for always being with me and protecting me because, frankly, I was not capable of protecting myself. Social interaction was, and still is, sometimes scary. However, as I have placed my trust in my Savior Jesus Christ, I realize that I have nothing to fear.

Prayer
God, You did not make me to fear. Yet, I do fear. Remove this infirmity from me so that I may face life as it presents itself.

Thought
Anxiety and stress raise the blood pressure and lead to headaches, heart attack, and other ailments. Take time to pray, and then let it go. Worry will not resolve anything. Have faith that the Lord will do what His living Word promises. He will carry us through. Even then it will not be painless, but watch and see that you will get through it by God's grace and help.

Scripture
"God has dealt to each one a measure of faith." (Rom. 12:3, NKJV)

Group/Individual Study

A. Begin with prayer.
B. Read the scripture.
C. Reflect on the scripture.
D. Answer the thought questions.

Thought Questions

1. Giving our concerns to God may be a novel idea for some, but does it truly resolve anything? Has it done so for you?

2. Why do we run from God? Do we not believe what He promises in His Word?

3. When we sin, is our temple desecrated, as the temple was desecrated when the temple's curtain was torn at Jesus' death? Why or why not?

4. Faith is the substance of things not seen. Is it easy to hold onto faith when the bill collector is knocking?

Day 5.

BROKEN

Fallen pieces, a mosaic of life
Swaths of patchwork cloth that divide.
Paths that lead through the wide gate
Familiar journey as we travel through space.

Shallow emptiness, a price so high,
Following empty paths cluttered with souls,
Reaching out for a hand to hold,
This broken path of the lonely and cold.

So many swaths, so much pain
So much trouble, the paths the same.
The wide gate, an easy journey
An exodus of souls, death to many.

Fallen pieces, the mosaic of life
Stitched together with the blood of Christ.
Wide is the gate that leads to death
A journey from God, a place not meant.

Reflection
In this world, there are so many groups, representing every imaginable way of thinking. All of these groups want to be influential over the masses. However, there are groups and elements of popular groups that are evil and that have an egocentric agenda. These groups prey on the innocent and weak, using propaganda that hides the truth.

When joining any group, we should ask ourselves why we are joining and what we can expect to gain from our participation. If we fail to ask ourselves these questions, we are prone to join for the wrong reason. In my own case, I often joined to gain popularity among my closest friends. Other times I joined because I accepted the suggestion of someone who thought it was a good thing. Nevertheless, whenever the full agenda is revealed, I quickly lose interest and leave the group.

Whenever I allow myself to get caught up in the enthusiasm of the moment, I usually find that I have signed a check that my body cannot cash. And that is when the nightmare begins. It is much simpler to take the time to do our homework first, instead of having to clean up afterwards. In all we do, we must keep God first, asking Him to guide us in all our affairs. We may not like the answer He gives us, but His promise is that He will never leave us nor forsake us.

Prayer
Dear God, Your Word says that You will never leave or forsake me. Today, Father, I am holding You to Your Word. If what I am requesting is Your will, then let it be done.

Thought
My mother always suggested that my siblings and I be leaders and not followers. However, leading others has its temptations and pitfalls. Leading others is wonderful when we allow God to lead us. Sometimes in leading others, the wide gate seems

much easier than the narrow one, even though choosing the wide gate often leads us down paths that cause us and others much pain.

Scripture
"Strive to enter through the narrow gate, for many, I say to you, will seek to enter and not be able." (Luke 13:24, NKJV)

Group/Individual Study

A. Begin with prayer.
B. Read the scripture.
C. Reflect on the scripture.
D. Answer the thought questions.

Thought Questions

1. In the book of Genesis, Adam and Eve fell from God's grace. How has this affected us today?

2. If God is perfect in power and wisdom and He freely desires to share these with us, why do we dismiss Him from our decision-making process? (When thinking about your answer, consider the story of Adam and Eve in the Garden with the serpent.)

3. Did Satan truly deceive humans, or are we, rather willing participants in sin, eager to utilize deception ourselves to get what we want without due consideration for sin's evil nature?

4. Remembering a wide gate in your life, was it easy or was it difficult to leave for the narrow gate of God?

Day 6.

SELF-DESTRUCTION

The unknown surrounds my life.
Spirit weakened, my mind remains strong.
God watches the horror, and He lets it be.
Choices given freely though they may kill me.

A week of seven days, God, You rested after six.
I find no peace in my space, or in my thoughts.
My weaknesses torment my conscience constantly.
Today, I dream, though success is hard to see.

Angels watch me freely fall from Thee.
The guiding steps made for me are but a dream.
My flesh, reckless, tries to destroy me.
The angels weep silently.

I continue my flight in life out of control.
Stability remembered, a stable time of joy.
A gift lost, images returning to me.
A weakened spirit looks towards home, steps ordered by Thee.

Self-Destruction

What is wrong with the creation God made in His image?
Satan's ability to kill is the will of the Creator.
A child lost must never give up looking for home.
God made me. Jesus saved me. My soul will not be lost.

Reflection

This poem further describes the back and forth of my addiction, my need to be a part of the popular group throughout the various stages of my life, and my later realization that individuality plays an important role in the development of character.

In the end, our behavior determines whether our circumstances destroy or humble us. Inevitably we are free to go in the direction of our choosing. I was caught up in behaviors that achieved nothing. Coupled with the selfishness of addiction, I was a mess.

The attraction of being like what I idolized was stronger than the pain that I suffered as a consequence of my destructive lifestyle. Therefore, I returned to my addiction multiple times before I hit bottom. I am grateful, however, that I recognized when I hit bottom and sought help. Many do not recognize or acknowledge the self-destructive nature of their behaviors and, therefore, continue down the path to an uncertain end.

Prayer

Lord, continue to demonstrate in me your spiritual gift of humility. Let my actions be an expression, a demonstration, and a testimony of salvation that can only come from You.

Thought

I believed that I knew my destiny, and I believed that it was up to me to achieve it by myself. What I discovered, after I crashed and burned, is this: "Your will be done, God."

Scripture

"Do not deliver me to the will of my adversaries; for false witnesses have risen against me, And such as breathe out violence. I would have lost heart, unless I had believed that I would see the goodness of the LORD in the land of the living." (Psalm 27:12, 13, NKJV)

Group/Individual Study

A. Begin with prayer.
B. Read the scripture.
C. Reflect on the scripture.
D. Answer the thought questions.

Thought Questions

1. Are we really in control of our destiny? or are our steps pre-determined by the path that we choose to follow?

2. Does pride inevitably lead to self-destruction?

3. Why is rebellion a self-destructive attitude?

4. Can rebellion be forgiven and should it? Why?

Day 7.

THE DOOR

Open the door to a space of darkness your own.
A zone, not home, a space to depart to, which welcomes no one but your soul,
Hiding from those who critique others as their mirror crashes.
People caught in their own throws.

Placing tags on those who hide from life,
While the truth that comes with sight is razed by the sighted,
Whose judgments dribble, like the flow on a pillow, the wet spot that soils the cloth.

For through the darkness, the light of truth can be gleaned,
Unlocking the door to the space that hides the view,
Protecting the soul from the spurious multitude, who besiege us few.

Falling to depths not clearly seen, for the judgments of others are heavy,
Wanting to be the self that God intended, yet not knowing how it could be,
Holding to His Word, and pushing it away believing it cannot be heard,

Retreating once more to the place not home, the dark space your own.

Short on integrity, a slow transition to happy ends,
Knowing He is there, though the choice of paths not clear.
The promise He can't break assures that He will turn the knob,
Unlocking the door to the dark place, the zone that hides your soul.

Reflection

This poem builds on the theme that what is hidden in darkness will come into the light. I have heard other addicts say that they believed no one knew what they were doing. But, when they became sober and listened to the truth, they discovered that everyone knew. I believed that I was so cunning, yet everyone had a general idea of what I was doing, even if they did not know the specifics. Only a handful knew the whole truth.

I began to recognize the hold that darkness had on me when my meekness became aggression in every aspect of my life. Years would go by before I accepted the decay of life that I was experiencing. The greatest of devastations to me was when my family members politely dismissed my presence, not knowing how I was going to act.

Today, in every way, I try to acknowledge God for keeping me through my darkness. I believe He walked with me and kept me during this period. How else could I have survived in my right mind and in relatively good health?

Prayer

Father, let the meditation of my thoughts, actions, and the love in my heart be a conduit that ignites another to open the door of their soul to invite You in.

Thought

Placing tags on people whether good or bad is not helpful. It hurts to discover that we have a label of judgment placed upon us, even when the label is deserving. Judgment is not for human beings. It is the exclusive dominion of God, which He has given to Christ Jesus when Jesus made His loving sacrifice of death for us all (John 5:22, 23).

Scripture
"You shall not pervert the judgment of your poor in his dispute. Keep yourself far from a false matter; do not kill the innocent and righteous. For I will not justify the wicked." (Exod. 23:6, 7, NKJV)

Group/Individual Study

A. Begin with prayer.
B. Read the scripture.
C. Reflect on the scripture.
D. Answer the thought questions.

Thought Questions

1. Personal perceptions of right and wrong will determine what we believe. Therefore, is our judgment of another person just a personal perception?

2. If the truth will set you free (John 8:32), then why is the truth feared?

3. How does the judgment of others affect our character?

4. When God opens the door to your soul, what will He see?

5. John the Baptist labored to lay the foundation for Jesus' arrival. Describe the darkness he labored in.

Day 8.

GREED

Young, no future seen.
Traditional learning boring not free.
Street life remains fluid always in motion.
Greed exceeds life, the vision of freedom.

Money is the object of my desire.
The riches gained by any means.
My greed grows enormously.
That green paper, it won't elude me.

A tree is milled to create it.
Give me the money or I'll take it.
It's what motivates me to live.
Never mind the danger, I'll seek more of it.

How far will I go to get it?
I will kill a man and watch him bleed.
Steal from a man, deny it was me.
Manipulate a man until he discovers it is gone.

No compassion is alive in me.
A spirit determined just to be free.
Structure exists only for the weak.
The streets, duplicity, are what I seek.

The whore drives man's greed.
Betrayal, not love, rewards in silver.
Jesus condemned through the price of a kiss.
Envision a noose, the sway of death.

Greed

Reflection

I survived the streets, running with drug dealers, users, prostitutes, and conmen. Though I did not participate in their activities at first, I was around them daily. Eventually, they let me into their world; I felt as if my life was full and free.

Interestingly, most of the street runners were half my age and believed that the life they were living was actually living. I knew better, and the quality of life I observed was degrading. Yet, the money they possessed opened my eyes wide. At times, I wanted to participate in the activities they were doing with the same vigor as they did. Yet, looking over my shoulder to watch my back on a minute-by-minute basis is not living. It is just survival.

They swindled their customers, each other, and plotted on a regular bases how they could increase their daily revenue. Some of them engaged in gunplay when they thought it necessary. Today, many years removed, I am thankful to say that the seduction of the fast life did not completely corrupt me or my values. God's loving arms were still around me. He never let me go.

Prayer

Jesus, hear my plea—may my love for You and the Father always exceed my desire for earthly things. Remove greed from my heart and thoughts. Replace them with love for my neighbor.

Thought

The one important lesson I learned on the street is that the street never loses. In life, God gives us a choice. We can choose to do right or we can choose to do wrong. Street life does not give that choice. Survival means doing whatever is necessary.

Scripture
"For the wicked boasts of his heart's desire; he blesses the greedy and renounces the LORD." (Psalm 10:3, NKJV)

Group/Individual Study

A. Begin with prayer.
B. Read the scripture.
C. Reflect on the scripture.
D. Answer the thought questions.

Thought Questions

1. The word "whore" was used in the poem symbolically. Who does the whore represent?

2. Money sustains every aspect of our lives. However, should money replace the mercy and grace a forgiving Father gives freely? Describe a situation in which the love of money is more important than the Father's eternal love.

3. We pursue life's amenities often with zeal. Do we seek God and our Savior with the same zeal or do we do so passively? Why is this?

4. Is money the root of evil? If you are not sure about the answer, consider Judas' desire to receive payment for his betrayal. What then was his motivation for the decision he made after he admitted betraying innocent blood?

Day 9.

DESIRE

Desire's faithfulness redirects God's love.
Her aim to serve the needs of the flesh.
Deceptive tactics target self-destruction.
Satan's love strengthens her will.

Her only concern is day descending to night.
The darkness of the night bears her strength.
Desire, a man will willfully follow,
Hiding wrongs tightly behind closed doors.

Images construed in the mind, not true.
Hearts filled with lustful anticipation.
Temptation smiles at victory at Satan's request.
Man separated from God's trust.

Desire medicates the soul of life.
She fills our hearts with gifts of joy,
Reaps excitement of danger through our veins,
Laughs at our Savior's love in vain.

Man will follow her to his own end,
Seeking her, Desire, she haunts our will.
Human flesh, the untold tally grows,
Leading us from God, Satan's death march goes.

Reflection

As a child, I wanted to be able to stay up late like the grown-ups. I believed that all the best programs came on after 7 p.m. When I became a teenager, I believed that I was already grown and could make my own decisions, never mind that I was still under my parents' roof.

"Desire" for me came in watching the pretty people, the cool people, with their multiple girlfriends, nice clothes, and fast talk. These people seemingly had it all together. I wanted what they had, never mind that it did not suit me because I actually enjoyed life, learning, and experiencing the beauty and history around me.

Living in the world and seeing its indulgences was overwhelming and enticing. Young and impressionable, I felt that I was missing out, a thought that is an egocentric and destructive path for those who follow the fantasy pathway of their associates. If we focus on that which is right and not on that which is popular or comfortable, desire and temptation to commit sinful acts will not be able to command our attention.

Prayer

Lord Jesus, guide me in all Your ways. Give me the courage not to accept the influences of the world around me.

Thought

Desire is an image of the mind that leads us to pursue outcomes that may bring pain and heartbreak. It is wanting what your neighbors have without understanding what they went through to get it.

Scripture

"But as for those whose hearts follow the desire for their detestable things and their abominations, I will recompense their deeds on their own heads." (Eze. 11:21, NKJV)

Desire

Group/Individual Study

A. Begin with prayer.
B. Read the scripture.
C. Reflect on the scripture.
D. Answer the thought questions.

Thought Questions

1. Jesus said that lust is a sin. If that is so, is desire like lusting and is desire also a sin?

2. Is it possible not to desire something that someone else may have?

3. Let us say that you desire something and then you actually get it. A week, a month, or a year later, was it worth the price you paid? How long did the newness or the appreciation of the acquisition last?

4. What we do in the darkness, the Bible says, will come into the light. Is this biblical statement true all the time, some of the time, or never?

Day 10.

CONFLICTED

With razed emotions, I failed.
The spirit within forgotten,
For the tempted soul struggles,
Grasps, yet finds nothing.

Aimless, the wind blows.
Its conviction of nothingness shows.
Satan draws near, as a spirit of air.
Reserves a place in man's ear.

The opposition, I covet.
The promises disregarded.
I wither once more.His crown found outside my door.

Why? You own the soul.
Exhausted, I run the treadmill.
Tired, though I continue to wonder.
The spaces empty of the soul.

Reflection
Imagine the devastation of homelessness, addiction, and alcoholism on the individual and the family. Ask yourself: Do the people trapped in these situations really want to live like this? They experience life that is difficult and degrading, often blaming others for their situation. They never ask themselves what role they are playing in their circumstances. Many blame the community and the government for their problems and then expect the same community and government to take care of them.

I recognize that, for me, it was pride and arrogance that led me to my circumstances. Add to these motivations the childhood trauma that I experienced, and the result was an angry man who was confused about himself and his purpose in life. Homelessness, jail, and addiction were a dark path. Yet, knowing God, I believed that He had the power to change me and my direction. All I had to do was to have faith and ask for His help. As I believed, I expected a change. As I diligently sought Him, I expected a change. As my faith grew, I expected a change. Then, what I expected came into existence because I believed.

Prayer
God, You changed my sentence through prayer. The word says, "Ask and you will receive." I am asking, Father, that You hear my prayer. Keep me on a path that leads only to the substantive truth in Your Word.

Thought
Remember the message that God gave Moses—the Ten Commandments. Their instruction is one of the keys to life for God's people. We need not live life aimlessly. God never

promised that we would never fail. However, when we put our burdens on Him, He fills the emptiness with a blessing that strips away our burdens and gives us peace.

Scripture

"If you do well, will you not be accepted? And if you do not do well, sin lies at the door. And its desire is for you, but you should rule over it." (Gen. 4:7, NKJV)

Conflicted

Group/Individual Study

A. Begin with prayer.
B. Read the scripture.
C. Reflect on the scripture.
D. Answer the thought questions.

Thought Questions

1. Can emotional stress lead us away from God? Why?

2. Describe a temptation that has led you away from God.

3. What do you covet?

4. Did God give every man a soul? What do you believe the soul is?

5. Is it God's will for us to fail?

6. What event acquainted humankind with failure?

Part 2
Spiritual Awakening

INCARCERATED FREEDOM, A PRISON STATE OF MIND

Prison was a familiar theme and experience for many biblical figures—from Joseph to Peter, Paul, Barabbas, Silas, and even John the Beloved. Yet, in most of the biblical examples of imprisonment, the incarcerated were innocent of the charges levied against them. Even today, one hears repeated jailhouse cries of innocence from the imprisoned. How many of those truly guilty of the crimes for which they were incarcerated face the truth of their transgressions? Even so, whether innocent or guilty, God the Father seems to have a special affection and concern for those who are imprisoned. David wrote about His concern: "To hear the groaning of the prisoner; to loose those that are appointed to death; ... for the LORD heareth the poor, and despiseth not his prisoners" (Psalm 102:20; 69:33).

Jesus commissioned His disciples to acquaint themselves with prisons and to visit those incarcerated in them frequently. Why would the spotless Lamb of righteousness, the only One to walk the earth without transgression or sin, ask his disciples through the ages to visit prisoners? "I the LORD have called thee in righteousness, and will hold thine hand, and will keep thee, and give thee for a covenant of the people, for a light of the Gentiles; to open the blind eyes, to bring out the prisoners from the prison, and them that sit in darkness out of the prison house" (Isaiah 42:6, 7).

Why? Because Christ is acquainted with all of our infirmities. "For Christ also hath once suffered for sins, the just for the unjust, that he might bring us to God, being put to death in the flesh, but quickened by the Spirit: By which also he went and preached unto the spirits in prison" (1 Peter 3:18, 19). It is not a coincidence that many prisoners come to know our Lord and Savior Jesus Christ in the cellblock. This is the very place that the Holy Spirit often works. Perhaps, it is the place where darkness finds light, confusion meets understanding, selfishness finds self-sacrifice, guilt finds forgiveness, bondage leads to surrender and surrender to freedom. "Our enemies may thrust us into prison, but prison walls cannot cut off the communication between Christ and our souls. One who sees our every weakness, who is acquainted with every trial, is above all earthly powers; and angels come to us in lonely cells, bringing light and peace from heaven" (Ellen G. White, *Gospel Workers* [1892], p. 424).

The writer of this book takes us on this very journey from prisoner to prisoner of Christ! It is a privilege to be shackled to Christ, to wear His prison garments, whether they are black and white stripes or orange jumpsuits. Paul and Silas prayed and sang songs of praise unto God, and all within the jailhouse heard them. Our Father also heard their prayers, and, in response, "the foundations of the prison were shaken: and immediately all the doors were opened, and every one's bands were loosed" (Acts 16:26).

Brian Wise
Elder Northeast SDA Church, Charlotte, North Carolina
Massachusetts Institute of Technology, Community Fellow, Department of Urban Studies
Colgate University, B.A. Economics

JAIL HOUSE POEMS

The following ten poems are the works I started and completed while I was incarcerated. The significance of these poems is that they helped me to come to terms with my substance abuse. Even though my incarceration was not due to drugs or the drug culture directly, I did have a problem. This open admission began the process of freeing my soul and taking my life back from the depths of hell that I had fallen into and from the mind-altering substances that controlled my thinking and behavior.

These poems also helped me to find personal forgiveness because I needed to forgive myself before I could ask the ones I had hurt to forgive me. My tendency toward addiction will be with me for as long as I live. However, today I have freedom, and a clear mind, to make decisions without the need of substances.

My hope for the reader is that, after reading my testimony, you will find solace in your situation and realize that using a substance—any substance—is not the answer to your problems. Bad things happen in life, and we need to responsibly ask ourselves what role we played in them. Then we need to seek spiritual guidance for the answer.

Day 11.

HALF SHADY

Demons lay siege to my life,
Diversion to God's glorious march.
Death knocks upon the door,
Pressing past the ramparts, against the sword.

Death will not tame the pain,
For evil's fast beautiful life I have pledged.
What they reap on the world, I now sow,
In symphonic pictorial prose.

Closed eyes reveal dark silky shadows,
Slithering along walls, doors, and matter.
This disease inside me shaking my soul
Awakens my heart, my weakness foretold.

For half the man that I am,
Ranging life's fence, to satisfy man
When Christ rode in fifteen thousand strong
I repented late, now hell is home.

Half Shady

He said, "Come to me with all your burdens."
I did so, half the man that I am,
Has given me a new address, not home,
But, an orange suit, with lights that burn on.

Reflection

Growing up, I saw plenty of sinful activities happening around me daily. The youth of my neighborhood engaged in drugs, alcohol, sex, and gambling. These were normal for me, and as such, I fell prey to that way of life. As I grew older, much of what I had participated in remained and became a part of my character. Though considered darkness and the underbelly of society, it became my alter-self. Those around me saw me as a real and not a fake person, though I acted one way for one group and a different way for another.

However, the Word of God declares: "No man can serve two masters" (Matt. 6:24). This is true, yet many people, including myself, have tried. We have consistently obtained the same results, the two worlds eventually collide. God gives us choices that are as easy as "yes" or "no," right or wrong. Nonetheless, the flesh, which is the devil's playground, tends to command our attention. The best that we can be is ourselves—sinners saved by grace.

Prayer

Father, please forgive me for not paying attention to You when You have spoken. Make my ears to hear Your mighty, merciful voice.

Thought

"To be alive is to be broken; to be broken is to stand in need of grace."

Scripture

"I say to you that likewise there will be more joy in heaven over one sinner who repents than over ninety-nine just persons who need no repentance." (Luke 15:7, NKJV)

Group/Individual Study

A. Begin with prayer.
B. Read the scripture aloud.
C. Reflect on the scripture.
D. Answer the thought questions.

Thought Questions

1. Demons lay siege; at times, life can seem overwhelming. Does the statement "demons lay siege" refer literally or figuratively to demons?

2. Does acceptance of the use of drugs and adultery in American culture mean that each individual who subscribes to this behavior is reaping what he or she has sown?

3. What does the orange suit in the poem represent?

Day 12.

PROPHETIC DREAM

Chair back against the painted wall,
He rests, white shorts, barefoot.
Yesterday's thoughts are feelings lost,
Streaming tears replace a loving heart.

Not clear why love deteriorated,
He studies his soul
Uncovered opportunities to fix the trend,
Neither he nor she called Him into their midst.

Cold steel fitting the right hand,
Rock-n-roll, the sound from the music box stand,
Sweet Home Alabama fills the soul.
Five o'clock strikes, awakening his confused soul.

Christ paid the ultimate price: death
Many feel trapped in their circumstance
Old or young, strife is strong, read the king's psalms
For David's praise shows a longing for God.

Prophetic Dream

The Lord is my shepherd I shall not want,
Reading on, he becomes enlightened,
Rising from the chair one minute past five,
Love being greater than death, hope lives on.

Reflection

Recently I had a dream that seemed quite real. It was vivid and deadly. A nightmare, it shook me to my core. I shared the dream with others, hoping to learn what it meant. All were amazed at the details I shared. However, they deciphered its meaning incorrectly. No one spent much time with me exploring its source.

In today's society, we are stretched in so many directions that we fail miserably in listening to one another and miss signs that could help a desperate soul. When things eventually do go wrong, we react in horror and separate ourselves from the person involved.

The nightmare I had was not physically fulfilled, yet I could see that it portrayed a spiritual death that I experienced, even though a physical event did occur eight days later. Many, at the time, separated themselves from me. Even those who heard the dream were slow to offer comforting words. We must always remember that, even when we feel abandoned, God is with us. His promise is: "I will never leave you nor forsake you."

Prayer

Gracious Father, allow me to help in another person's time of need. Allow me to be a loving reflection of You whenever needed.

Thought

Never be too busy to help your brother. Remember, you *are* your brother's keeper.

Scripture

Jesus Christ nailed to the wood has carried our pain into the peace of grace. He has "made peace through the blood of His Cross." (Col. 1:20, NKJV)

Group/Individual Study

A. Begin with prayer.
B. Read the scripture aloud.
C. Reflect on the scripture.
D. Answer the thought questions.

Thought Questions

1. Suicide is a damning expression of helplessness, however, does it solve our problems or does it only postpone them for someone else?

2. The willingness to share what we are feeling, when we are in the grip of pain is difficult. Does communicating our pain to someone else help or hinder?

3. Do we really believe God's promise that "He will never leave us," or is that just a comforting statement?

Day 13.

THE PRISONER

Shades of orange blanket the floor,
Covering the willing and the scared.
Fluorescent lights burn all the day,
As ministers protect each guilty life.

Finding nothing wrong here, just more fear,
Freedoms locked away for years.
Here we be clad in orange suits;
Men domiciled behind iron and brick.

Captured, we live free of freedom's work,
Watching what free men do.
While the clock of routine movements passes us by—
Tick on, tick tock, lights out or on.

Chained to sin, reaching for freedom's limb,
Evildoers, not life takers, the ultimate sin,
Brushing off demons devouring the flesh,
Breaking chains that bind us to where we exist.

The Prisoner

Darkness and life are not one and the same
In this place where life isn't sane.
Laughter and smiles because life goes on here,
Counting the days as freedom nears.

Reflection

Hanging out on the street, I often heard off-the-wall stories, which were often embellishments of the truth. The stories that always intrigued me most were those that described jail life. Perhaps they were so intriguing because I never imagined myself ever being behind bars.

Today, no longer intrigued, I am the character in the stories shared on the corner. Jail is not a fun place at all. In fact, it's a little scary. It is living under the restriction of the freedom of choice and under someone else's command . When I was young, my mother often told me to engage my brain before my mouth. I ended up going to jail because I failed to heed her instructions. I brought on my own loss of freedom. Better decisions would have allowed for better choices. Yet, God still loves me.

Adam and Eve were given the opportunity to choose, and their poor decision gave rise to the many poor decisions that we still make today. The Bible tells us that we cannot serve two masters, for we will eventually choose one over the other. Because of God's mercy, free people are given many choices. Which ones we make eventually determines the path in life we ultimately follow.

Prayer

Lord Jesus, teach me how to call upon Your grace and mercy when the trails of life besiege me. Show me how to wait quietly until You arrive.

Thought

Be careful about what you ask for, because the surroundings you seek may not be the ones you sought.

Scripture

"For he is God's minister to you for good. But if you do evil, be afraid; for he does not bear the sword in vain; for he is God's minister, an avenger to execute wrath on him who practices evil." (Rom. 13:4, NKJV)

Group/Individual Study

A. Begin with prayer.
B. Read the scripture aloud.
C. Reflect on the scripture.
D. Answer the thought questions.

Thought Questions

1. Are we trapped by our situation, or have we just given in to it?

2. Can a person be chained to circumstance?

3. Scripture states that God grants authority to civil servants. Do you agree?

Day 14.

SENTENCED

Diminished sight, cold cell lonely night.
On my way to prison, I crashed.
After I married, started a business,
Became the addict I am.

Do not judge me, for judgment is not yours,
The orange, actually looks good, bold.
In this fortress of kings, with burning lights,
Condemned men wait judgment's turn.

This truth is mine, I have forgiven me,
But I have been set aside to glorify He
who restores humility before His court.
As I sit lonely, hungry, and cold,
In need of nutrition, I feed on His Word.

With solitude and a clear mind,
I've rediscovered God, Christ, and His Bride—
The church, my loving family.
That's twice I've been denied.

Who am I to judge? He died to save me.
Forgiveness hurts to the point that you bleed.
Sorrow and pain, He suffered.
Man's rebuke is light upon me.

Reflection

Have you ever felt that God allowed a situation to occur to get your attention, to get you to hear God's Word? Jesus said: "My mother and my brothers are these who hear the word of God and do it" (Luke 8:21, NKJV).

After I was incarcerated, God got my attention. I pretended not to be shaken the first nine nights. However, on the tenth night, I wept. I remember awakening the next morning, feeling that something had changed in my spirit. The sun filtered into my cell that morning, and I felt free. The burdens that I had been hauling around seemed to have fallen away.

An ease came over me that I had not felt in years. God sometimes needs us to change address, whether we want to or not. He wants our attention, our love. He wants a personal relationship with us, His children. So, be still and listen for Him. His Word says that He will never leave us nor forsake us.

Prayer

Father God, may the best that You have planned for me be realized in Your time, according to Your wishes.

Thought

Study and meditate on the word of God.

Scripture

"For which I suffer trouble as an evildoer, even to the point of chains; but the word of God is not chained." (2 Tim. 2:9, NKJV)

Group/Individual Study

A. Begin with prayer.
B. Read the scripture aloud.
C. Reflect on the scripture.
D. Answer the thought questions.

Thought Questions

1. It is commonplace for people to label or judge the actions of another. Is it possible, as human beings, not to judge or have an opinion?

2. Is having an opinion a judgment and wrong?

3. After asking for forgiveness, is it fair to expect reconciliation immediately?

4. If an apology is offered and accepted, how long does the recipient have to show true acceptance?

Day 15.

SOCIETY'S ONE VEST

Orange cotton threads surround each man.
Kings, clad in orange, upon thrones of guilt,
Existing as strangers in the same peel,
Whose deeds have crossed society's vest?

Statistics reveal education the means,
Exhortation, the path for those who succeed.
Some desire the easy route,
Thus, they twerk and jerk just to be seen.

A dance with God is ridiculed and shamed,
While sinners proclaim pretending is game.
Accepting worldly truth as the gospel,
Gained each sinner a just fame.

For "wisdom is justified of her children."
For sin is the world, not the world within.
They share a common peel by circumstance.
Imitated paths chase a common decent.

The temple stands as a fortress of life.
Pillars fall, bringing destruction and strife, thus,
Praise the difference that we each process.
For, the journey of life begins in society's one vest.

Reflection

Many years ago, I went to a weekend party of young people. The music and the crowd were loud and unruly. One group of young men from a different community arrived at the party, itching to create trouble. They were not welcomed, and one of them lashed out. A while later, a young man lay dead in the street, shot to death.

Every day we must deal with differences of opinion. However, the commission of a crime of this magnitude only destroyed the lives of two young men. We should be merciful in our actions, as God is merciful to us. He offered His Son as a ransom for our sins. Taking a life for any reason is senseless. God told the Israelites that it is a sin to spill blood. Murder cuts a person off from the community.

Just as man has created laws to maintain order, so did God create His law to govern human behavior. He also ordains leaders to govern. Therefore, we are to respect their leadership. If we fail to follow the law, there will be consequences.

Prayer

Abba Father, allow my actions to bring glory to Your name in love, joy and hope. Let those who witness my actions know the graciousness of my God.

Thought

Society says all people deserve a second chance, but the reality in society is that it depends on who the person is who is being offered the chance! I have learned from experience that all men are *now* equal in society.

Scripture

"The Son of Man has come eating and drinking, and you say 'Look, a glutton and a winebibber, a friend of tax collectors and sinners!' But wisdom is justified by all her children." (Luke 7:34, 35, NKJV)

Group/Individual Study

A. Begin with prayer.
B. Read the scripture aloud.
C. Reflect on the scripture.
D. Answer the thought questions.

Thought Questions

1. The rule of law guides the decisions that are adjudicated daily. However, many feel that the laws are skewed. Do you think that the application of law is skewed?

2. If skewed, how does it affect our families, communities (including the races), and our nation?

3. What is wisdom? How do we get it? How do we apply it in our daily lives?

4. What does the phrase "society's one vest" mean?

Day 16.

LINES OF INSANITY

A melancholy soul leaves the heart exposed.
Heap of sadness a touch of despair,
A collision of matter rains in the air.
Aggression soon slashes at God's love affair.

Prophecy foretells these mini stories,
No holding enforced, no action intended.
A measure of hope, prayer is added.
Yet, selfish intentions bring the "I" to stand.

Outrage brings separation and anger,
Damning the feeling failure brings.
Two hearts lay broken and exposed.
One free, both lay lonely.

A phenomenon fueled by anguish and grief,
For no action by one, damns a community.
Too busy to recognize a troubled soul,
Destroyed, confused incapable of letting go.

A vicious cycle of human emotions,
Humility surrendered to keep appearances,
Love of family, friends, and extended loved ones,
Morning may bring disappointments to bear.

Reflection

It is not funny to hear someone being called "crazy" because they behave differently or hold a different set of beliefs. Yet, people are often marginalized for seeing the world differently or for being willing to take a risk on their beliefs. What is funny is the cliché, "You have to spend money to earn money." Is this not a description of risk taking in the world's financial markets? We read *The Wall Street Journal* and other financial literature to make informed financial "bets" on the future. Yet, people are ridiculed for taking the risk of publicly acknowledging different informed beliefs.

Jesus took a risk when he appeared in the flesh. Though prophecy had foretold His coming and a multitude of prophets announced His coming to the masses, when He came, the people did not recognize Him. He was different from what they wanted. Ultimately, He was put to death by the very hands of those He came to save.

In our busy world, we have many demands upon our attention. Yet, we should not forget the single-most important law ever given to us: "You shall love your neighbor as yourself" (Matt. 19:19, NKJV). Differences have made American society one of the greatest in the world. Let us cherish our differences and stop attacking one another for them.

Prayer

Father God, I pray for all the people around the world who are sick and shut in. I pray that they may receive a blessing of mercy for better health. I also pray that we may display more love toward one another and cherish peace for all mankind.

Thought

Be mindful of the situations over which you have no control so that you do not allow them to overwhelm you with stress.

Scripture

"No one, when he has lit a lamp, puts it in a secret place or under a blanket, but on a lamp stand, that those who come in may see the light." (Luke 11:33, NKJV)

Group/Individual Study

A. Begin with prayer.
B. Read the scripture aloud.
C. Reflect on the scripture.
D. Answer the thought questions.

Thought Questions

1. Aggression affects people differently, but is it demonic?

2. Actions bring about either a positive or a negative result. Is procrastination more acceptable than not letting things fall through? Is it the norm?

3. Are we blind to what is happening in our community, or are we simply choosing to look the other way?

4. If we are choosing to look away, are we not then responsible for the negative consequences of the actions that we have ignored?

Day 17.

INFECTIOUS BEAUTY

Dinner arrived, dashed intentions.
The odor of fish, a life defined.
An image, an unsavory look,
At Satan, the walk he took.

Returning the meal, the server utters,
Radiant, complete savory appearance.
The payment of the previous plate.
The image of life so full of hate.

Adduced image spoiled the dish.
Succulent image of white finned fish.
The gills brought an anxious moment to bear.
The thin lines in our conscience became clear.

Able to create a smooth silky walk,
Devious image of self, a life with guilt,
Crushing hopes, dashing praise,
Walk with pride, a fall from favor.

Honesty sets free a remorseful soul.
Scared dead spirits long for freedom's shore.
Choosing wisely what you sow, for you will reap.
Yielding is better than searching for Me.

Reflection

As a young, impressionable child, I was mocked for having buckteeth. The taunting I received came from the white kids as well as the black ones, including my siblings.

Peer pressure over appearance was daunting. My mother understood this and encouraged me to laugh. She told me that, if I laughed at myself, then all that the others could do would be to laugh with me. Over time, I embraced my differences and used them to excel at other challenges. Nonetheless, it was not easy, and the scars have lasted through the years.

The differences that exist in society can either strengthen or weaken it. In the movie "The Truman Show," society was artificially portrayed as weirdly uniform and happy all the time. Of course, it is not. Not all differences are of equal value. We determine a tree's value by its fruits (Matt. 7:18–20). We overcome the difficulties of diversity by communicating with one another. Ridicule only wastes time and energy. I struggled with an inferiority complex for much of my adult life. Yet, now I have learned to accept my differences and have grown to value them.

Prayer

Lord, teach me to accept Your design, the perfect image that You designed, regardless of whether or not anyone else sees the beauty in me.

Thought

Coming to terms with the truth is a necessity, but wallowing in the aftermath is not.

Scripture

"For we must all stand before Christ to be judged. We will each receive whatever we deserve for the good or evil we have done in this earthly body." (2 Cor. 5:10, NLT)

Group/Individual Study

A. Begin with prayer.
B. Read the scripture aloud.
C. Reflect on the scripture.
D. Answer the thought questions.

Thought Questions

1. The last time that you were served a meal that did not look appealing, describe what emotions and feelings you experienced.

2. Would you say that the emotions you felt were godly feelings? Or were they ungodly feelings that invoked a sense of anger?

3. Do you find it necessary to accept your role in an action, even if it leaves you feeling guilty?

4. If the result of a decision has left you feeling guilty, can you ask for forgiveness without making amends?

Day 18.

FORGIVE ME

From compassion springs forth love.
Caterpillars change to butterflies.
Spring beautifies the land and heart.
I and my neighbor exist as one.

Love is not an error, but incarnate,
For philosophy cannot explain the truth.
But in God, the lie dies.
Is truth an error, or is it a lie?

Hope brings a new narrative to spring.
Couples confess their love, with a ring.
Blissful love now in one accord,
Not divisible before God's love.

Believing in empty space, feeling sane,
Faith can restore all things.
Let His death not be in vain.
Christ's resurrection, the Trinity, the same.

Forgive Me

For I know love, self-destruction, and guilt;
It alters life and changes a man's course.
Yet, grace delivers freedom freely;
With love, I forgive me.

Reflection

Self-destruction at any level causes enormous pain to everyone we love. The acronym, HALT, illustrates how this behavior can be spotted in an individual. HALT stands for "**H**ungry, **A**ngry, **L**onely, and **T**ired." All these emotions can lead a person into a self-destructive mode.

Recalling my own self-destructive moments provides me insight into understanding the truth of the HALT acronym. Anger triggered the emotion and the physical trauma that ensued. I acted without thinking, without considering the consequences, and my life was changed forever.

However, in prayer, God can help what seems impossible. By setting self aside by being willing to let go of our will to His, God can remove the emotional distress from the equation. In Him we find solace, unabridged and everlasting. The emotions of HALT rarely resolve an issue. Conversely, focusing on the Lord allows us to ask for HELP, an acronym for **H**e **E**mits **L**ove **P**urposely.

Prayer

Father, forgive me; teach me how to forgive myself and to forgive others as You have forgiven us all.

Thought

No matter the nature of the trespass, or whether you have also been trespassed by the other person, always look first to forgive.

Scripture

"For as many as have not seen my face in the flesh, that their hearts may be encouraged, being knit together in love, and attaining to all riches of the full assurance of understanding, to the knowledge of the mystery of God, both of the Father and of Christ." (Col. 2:1, 2, NKJV)

Group/Individual Study

A. Begin with prayer.
B. Read the scripture aloud.
C. Reflect on the scripture.
D. Answer the thought questions.

Thought Questions

1. Why should we love our neighbor as our self?

2. If we can forgive our neighbor, shouldn't forgiving ourselves be easy?

3. When many scientists continue to dispute the truth of the Bible, can we consider the Bible a legitimate document?

4. Think of a time that you self-destructed. Describe it if you feel comfortable doing so.

Day 19.

REAL MEN

Real men love Christ, and the bride.
Their meekness misread as a weakness.
Real men cry out for the love of Him,
By whom I am governed and sentenced.

Real men cry, though it's not often heard,
Suffering silently, they hold on,
Enduring the pains of life and home.
A spiritual wife intercedes to God.

Rolling waves crash the cranium.
A life of absurdities surrounds him.
Thin lines lie between life and death,
For God's love justifies all that he risks.

Real men rejoice, I know, for I am one
Tears help to keep men strong
They open windows to God's loving will
Where results are complete and strong.

Real Men

Real men do cry for the love of God,
Diminished by those who own their own will,
Real men do cry for God revealed.
When the need is to have faith and be still.

Reflection
When I was a child, I behaved as a child; when I became a man, I had to let go of childish behaviors (1 Cor. 13:11). That is easier said than done. It is funny how simple sayings carry such power. The reality is that some of the childish behaviors that we adults want to run from are the very ones that make us human.

As a boy, I tried to hide my tears. Displaying tears could make survival in the projects a tough challenge. Knowing this, if I cried, I would try to stay away from others until the tears dried up. The only problem was that the red eyes from crying remained, and I did not realize this at first. When I did, I learned to suppress my emotions and hide my crying. Even today many feel that I am cold or unemotional because I have developed body language that hides my emotions.

Yet—news flash, folks—men do cry! The unresolved emotional baggage that I have carried through the years has weighed me down. Today, I don't call it emotional; I call it sentimental crying. Either way, it is the same thing.

How much baggage are you carrying? All of us would be better served if we would let it out. Perhaps then we would be able to release the stresses that are holding onto us. Perhaps it would create a kinder us, able to love and respect others and better equipped to follow through with the second great commandment to "Love your neighbor as yourself."

Prayer
God, may I begin all of my searching with prayer, so that the outcomes will be what You have planned for me according to Your wisdom and knowledge.

Thought
Men, it is all right to cry unto the Lord. Cry aloud, for it shows that you are human, with real emotions and real pain.

Scripture
"The God of my strength, in whom I will trust; my shield and the horn of my salvation, my stronghold and my refuge; my Savior, You save me from violence. I will call upon the LORD, who is worthy to be praised; so shall I be saved from my enemies." (2 Sam. 22:3, 4, NKJV)

Group/Individual Study

A. Begin with prayer.
B. Read the scripture aloud.
C. Reflect on the scripture.
D. Answer the thought questions.

Thought Questions

1. All small children cry—including boys. Is it okay for a man to cry?

2. When you see a man crying, what are your initial thoughts? Are there other thoughts that come to mind after that?

3. Why does it seem that men rely on themselves when they need help, and not on God or anyone else?

4. Women seem to be more in touch with their emotions than men. Is this because it is considered weakness for men to show emotion in public?

Day 20.

CHASING GRATITUDE

Tears of happiness fall, soft and wet,
Fleeting sentiments of a gathered joy.
Remembering a brokenness of endearing times,
Pursuing footprints destined for victory.

Overcoming death's place of prideful existence,
Gazing into a mirror, a look upon a lonely soul,
Focused upon a single voice, a single point of view.
A frightened child, unable to give another his due.

A diseased mind, stunted growth,
Wallowing in a world of make believe.
Search to free the pain locked inside,
Nirvana flees, as it laughs at me.

A world without gratitude, lost and cold.
The high cost of living low.
A chase for a ghost called happiness,
Who exists behind dark doors closed to me.

The Father's gift—the lamb is dead.
His blood flowed free to free my soul.
Prophetic dream of sentiments,
A cost so high pride releases me.

Humility lives in the person of God,
Dashing death's knock at my door.
His mercies offered when surrender is given,
Gratitude lives behind heaven's doors.

Reflection
The message of the cross releases from the pain of guilt and the tyranny of pride.

Prayer
Father God, why did it take me so long to see Your grace and respond to Your love? Let me never forget what You have done to redeem my life!

Thought
Feeling "death" led me to recognize my need of Jesus. Thank God for Calvary! Thank God for the gift of salvation!

Scripture
"But God forbid that I should glory except in the cross of our Lord Jesus Christ, by whom the world has been crucified to me, and I to the world." (Gal. 6:14, NKJV)

Group/Individual Study

A. Begin with prayer.
B. Read the scripture aloud.
C. Reflect on the scripture.
D. Answer the thought questions.

Thought Questions

1. What experience do you think the author is describing?

2. What does he mean by "chasing gratitude"?

3. Why do you suppose this poem follows the reflection on crying?

4. What is significant about chasing gratitude instead of chasing dreams?

Part 3
Life after Death

WOW—WHAT A JOURNEY!

Douglas Boyer has written his life's journey in retrospect. Through poetic reflection, he mysteriously draws the reader into his world. Decades of escaped emotions are relived. Dreams of a lost journey seem so far out of reach.

Yet, in the darkness, every fiber of our being seems to be stretched in resistance to the inevitable. Darkness is the futility of trying. It is thinking that everything and everyone is against us and nothing seems to be working for us. One taste of bittersweet darkness stifles our breath as we strain toward a single glimmer of light.

Boyer's writing reflects the dissatisfaction of the pain that comes from laboring through the change of lifestyle in which we have become entangled. Dark habits hold us back. At the very moment it appears that we will become overwhelmed and sucked into nothingness, hope springs eternal. Somewhere in the distance, a glimmer of light appears through the darkness, beckoning us to move forward (Luke 1:79), to place one foot in front of the other. Indeed, where there is light, there is victory, freedom, and hope.

Then, one day God appears in palpable light, extending His hand in our direction. He speaks softly and utters the words: "You have tried everything that you know. You have exerted all the will you can muster, and, yet, you are no farther along than when you began. Follow Me. Come, follow Me (John 12:26)."

For the first time, as we reach bottom in our frightened, miserable, and lonesome condition, we find ourselves experiencing real freedom, real hope, and real power of choice. What a journey!

Thank God for loving those who feel unlovable! Thank God for saving us and adopting us into His family!

And thank you, Douglas, for sharing your journey with us.

William L. Johnson Sr.
Elder Northeast SDA Church, Charlotte, North Carolina
Master Business Administration
Columbia University

THE JOURNEY

The poems in this section represent the start of a new journey. It is a journey in which I am free to express my emotions without anger and accepting where I am. It is a journey toward truth in my Christian walk, recognizing the "old man" and testifying against him. In the story I tell, the realities fall short of what I actually experienced. Yet, as I sought and received treatment for my addiction, the truth revealed itself. I experienced all the documented stages of the destructive and progressive behaviors of addiction and alcoholism.

For me, the trauma of ridicule drove the emotion of love from me and replaced it with anger. I turned to sports to express that anger. It worked for a while. Yet, something was still lacking: the anger then manifested itself in pride. I had to prove to everyone that I was better at everything that I aspired to do. This was the birth of my sinful behaviors.

I journeyed along this path until God showed me the bottom. Only God could have done this. I already believed that God is real; I just did not want to fully acknowledge Him—especially under the influence of my addiction. Today, I am grateful that His intimate design for me meant that He knew I would come home. This was to happen in His time and not in mine. I am blessed that He walked with me through it all.

Day 21.

DAY DREAM

Summer winds softly douse the body,
With warm waters from a summer rain.
Blissful thoughts of a time passed by—
Youthful love, giggles, laughter, and smiles.

Walking hand-in-hand in youthful bliss.
The age of knights on thunderous crusades.
Victorious rides under canopy arches of vegetation.
Medieval coronations like those in books.

Holding hands as sword-to-sword our crowns,
God observes our court, life all around, yet we fail.
Passing time, blood-red eyes of worry, absorbed in "I,"
Left hand filled with tissue, right hand raised to God asking, "Why?"

Precious man, no audible answer is heard,
For from the depths of the watery grave Your answer comes.
Lilies, birds, and all creatures worry not.
As faith rises, blessings descend as the summer rain.

Reflection

Recently I found a photograph that should never have been misplaced. It was a wedding photo of my wife and me. It was a memorable day, a happy time, right? Yes, it was memorable, but I am not sure about happy. Truthfully, I do not remember much about the day except that I married my beautiful wife. I was so messed up mentally that, if it were not for the picture I have to jog my memory, it would have been just another day.

Today, I think about that period of our lives, and I wonder what pain I brought into her life because of the pain I was already living with. Recognizing the origin of my strife and how it manifested itself in the uncontrollable monster that it became, serves as a testimony. When I observe people experiencing similar tragedies, I cannot help but wonder if their story is the same as mine. In many ways, I am sure it is. When pain is internalized, it manifests itself in horrifying ways.

Our thoughts can reflect our positive and negative realities. If our thoughts have the power to shape the way we see reality, then God must also have access to the shaping of reality, for, after all, He did create us. Wherever our minds go, He goes with us. My aim now is to keep my mind on getting it right today. I cannot fix the past. The past is the past, not my present nor the future God wants for me.

Thought

Our thoughts can take us to the places of our dreams. Depending on our circumstances and the possibilities of our socio-economic class, these dreams may be healthy or they may not. However, if we keep our focus on God and trust in His Word, both our daydreams and our night dreams will be healthy extensions of the reality He has in mind for us.

Prayer
Father, let my focus be on You, that, as I go through each day and night, my thoughts will be pleasing to You and serve the greater good of Your kingdom.

Scripture
"But first seek the kingdom of God and His righteousness, and all these things shall be added to you. Therefore do not worry about tomorrow, for tomorrow will worry about its own things. Sufficient for the day is its own trouble." (Matt. 6:33, 34, NKJV)

Group/Individual Study

A. Begin with prayer.
B. Read the scripture aloud.
C. Reflect on the scripture.
D. Answer the thought questions.

Thought Questions

1. Weddings are a memorable and happy time for the guests. Describe the level of stress you experienced (or imagine what it might be) in planning and going through your wedding.

2. Does your wedding photo display true happiness?

3. If married more than ten years, do you and your spouse still experience youthful giggles?

4. Reflect on a time when you had one hand filled with tissue and the other raised to God asking, "Why?"

Day 22.

WHY?

Old tree, standing healthy and tall.
Nurtured life-long trust,
Deep roots will bear weight.
I Am, though you must have faith.

The tree weathers storms unlike man,
For the flesh seeks freedom from Thee.
Fortify me. How do I pursue Thee
Unless I meditate?

Why must I wait? Why must You hesitate?
High Priest make me a way.
The pull of the flesh supports the death of the heart.
Grant me witness, show Your glory.

Earth, the carnage of death all around,
Fought on two fronts—in the spirit and on the ground.
Warfare that determines the destiny of each soul.
A fight, a choice, God chooses not to oppose.

Why?

The oak tree stands in silent conviction,
A beacon, a visible tower of strength,
Standing upright, strong in faith and the Word,
Protecting its heart, a living soul.

Reflection

The institution of marriage is ordain by God. It is a sacred commitment that is supposed to stand the test of time. "Supposed to," I say, because in the United States it seems that marriage is more a tool of convenience than the sacred institution God intended. Like the old oak tree, my marriage has stood for over a decade through turmoil, trials, and heartache. Wow, what a thought!

During that short time, we have witnessed the separation of all of our closest couple friends, a two-term Black American President, and Bible prophecy revealing itself before our eyes as the ISIS revolution has attempted to replace God on earth in the Middle East. Bible prophecy is upon us; we should stand for the truth.

The Bible says that we are to be soldiers for Christ, standing tall in the Word of truth. Don't be fooled. Many will try to convince you by quoting a verse or two. But, how are they living? How do they talk, walk, eat, and work? Would you permit your child to attend a slumber party at their house? Bible prophecy is upon us; I will be standing with Jesus.

Thought

Philanthropy is a blessing in the world. However, unless you have money to give away, you can scratch that idea. Yet, helping in whatever manner you can—in a soup kitchen or a homeless shelter or as a volunteer giving back to your community—means just as much to someone in need. Please consider volunteering.

Prayer

Jesus, Your message that the first shall be last and the last shall be first is a message of service. Lord, give me a heart and a desire to serve.

Scripture
"Then He arose and rebuked the wind, and said to the sea, 'Peace, be still!' And the wind ceased and there was a great calm. But He said to them, 'Why are you so fearful? How is it that you have no faith?' " (Mark 4:39, 40, NKJV).

Group/Individual Study

A. Begin with prayer.
B. Read the scripture aloud.
C. Reflect on the scripture.
D. Answer the thought questions.

Thought Questions

1. Soldiers stand tall; the old oak tree stands mighty. Will you stand tall for God no matter what circumstance comes before you? (Before answering consider what risks they must endure—the soldier stands in the line of fire, and the tree faces the lumberjack's saw.)

2. What does Christianity mean to you?

3. Name an event in the news that suggests that Bible prophecy is being fulfilled?

4. Does the event in your answer to question 3 correspond to the statement, "Earth, the carnage of death all around, fought on two fronts—in the spirit and on the ground"?

Day 23.

VICTORIOUS

Red strained eyes of sadness,
The craving greater than He arranged,
Trembling hands search for answers—
A win today or I fall away.

Self-imposed isolation, a ghastly change,
An idle mind sows opportunity for gain,
While mind traps accomplish nothing,
Burning desire no longer a strain.

Anguish fills the weary image of life,
Diminished in the furnace of the mind.
Recycled visions, moments for victory,
Uplifted, forgotten, and diluted dreams.

Into the light the unseen awaits
In the darkness sails conviction.
Rudderless futility steers aimlessly,
Discovering faith along the way.

Wickedness bows when challenged.
Gratitude ordains the path of life.
Insight is daunting without guidance.
Victory is sustained when God is raised.

Reflection

In any struggle for supremacy, there is the back and forth—the give and take—of defeat and victory. In every aspect of our lives, human emotions are affected and drawn into the conflict. It is a conflict that has many names and faces and always the same outcome—a loser or a winner.

Overcoming the pull of substance abuse—regardless of what that substance may be—is a monumental task. Victory does not come overnight. Relapses, no matter the substance, begins with just a thought. A reservation is (holding out thinking, "I want to quit," but choosing not to.), a challenge that beseiges the suffering addict. Sadly, some of those who relapse never make it back. They suffer the greatest of all losses—life.

We should give our full support to any brother or sister who is endeavoring to recover from substance abuse. God sacrificed His only Son for this objective. Jesus did not come to judge the world, but to save it. When we save one person, we can celebrate a victory, because one saved is one less lost.

Thought

Every day we face challenges that test our moral character. The ability to choose is a gift that God gives each one of us. Yet, there are many countries around the globe that restrict their citizens' choices. I thank God that I live in the United States of America.

Prayer

Lord, thank You for choice. I pray that, before making any decision, I will choose to come to You first, for You are God. You made me and have numbered my steps. Therefore, I say, may Your will be done.

Scripture
"Mark the blameless man, and observe the upright; for the future of that man is peace. But the transgressors shall be destroyed together; the future of the wicked shall be cut off." (Psalm 37:37, 38, NKJV)

Group/Individual Study

A. Begin with prayer.
B. Read the scripture aloud.
C. Reflect on the scripture.
D. Answer the thought questions.

Thought Questions

1. Jesus just let me hold on a little longer, I know it'll get better?

    A. Does it get better?

    B. How does it affect our faith? Do we thank Him, or do we curse Him?

2. Jesus commanded His followers to "Make disciples of all," which means to make them students of His. Are we victorious when we only make duplicates of ourselves?

    A. What about your adversary?

    B. What about the addict/alcoholic?

    C. What about the transient?

Day 24.

SOLUTIONS

Imagine going from saint to sinner,
Falling through space and time.
Through dark holes without a parachute—
Trails evil hearts often find.

A world where evil crowns reign,
The limits of shame our minds explore,
Jousting for position a way of survival.
We smile going home and cry on arrival.

Misunderstandings flank our attention;
Microwave needs demand our thoughts.
The Bible bread shares morality in stories,
Kneading dough characterizes mankind.

The sinner's spirit dwells in dark spaces.
Purgatory lives till truth arrives,
For freedom lives, abounding in knowledge.
He yearns for a covenant that lasts for all time.

Reflection
My childhood was rocky with craters and filled with mines. This was not because of what my mother did to me. I love my mother, and I thank God for her. However, parenting four children alone must have been a great challenge. That said, trouble seemed to follow me wherever I went. And I was a good kid!

I was the honor student who got caught viewing pornography in elementary school. I was the honor student/athlete in high school who spent time in detention for fighting each year. I was a kind person 99% of the time, yet, sometimes, I would allow my emotions to get the best of me. It seemed like I would be in free fall all school year, then that trap would open up, and I would just naturally step in.

Traps, black holes, whatever they are called, we all have them. Staying away from the edge and, more importantly, not falling in is what matters. We do this by finding an inner peace to guide, restrain, and refocus our energy. I discovered this truth late in life, and now I am sharing it with anyone and everyone who will listen. The wisdom of the Bible is over 2000 years old. However, it is still relevant because nothing has changed with regard to human behavior. We have just gotten a little sicker, and now we are even late arriving to the party!

Thought
Every organization we join has a statement that defines its purpose. Our membership means that we follow these organizational rules either intentionally or blindly. However, when God gave us the Ten Commandments, His laws for righteous living, it is too much. It is life or death. You get to choose.

Prayer

Father God, let Your law in my heart be a guiding light in my life. May I live a righteous life to the best of my ability, and, if I fall short, please forgive me of that sin.

Scripture

"And Moses said to the people, 'Do not fear; for God has come to test you, and that His fear may be before you, so that you may not sin.'" (Exod. 20:20, NKJV)

Group/Individual Study

A. Begin with prayer.
B. Read the scripture aloud.
C. Reflect on the scripture.
D. Answer the thought questions.

Thought Questions

1. Describe the meaning of the line, "A world where evil crowns reign."

2. What does the author mean by the phrase "microwave needs"?

3. The poem "Solutions" contains the couplet: "The Bible bread shares morality in stories, kneading dough characterizes mankind." Is the author using his own parable to describe man's behavior?

4. Describe your life trap? Has it ever swallowed you up?

5. Emotions, when left unchecked, can be a dangerous personal flaw in our character. How does the Bible help us to overcome our flaws?"

Day 25.

DANIEL 4

I, like Kings, unwilling to bow,
View a mirrored image of one
High on self-indulgence.
With no kingdom, no royal community—
Soul of dogged lost kings.

Not unintelligent, but prideful,
Not better, but bitter for the heckling,
I will exploit your desires,
Experience your dreams,
You who seek to be popular.

I lie in humility,
Walking fields of blacktop pavement.
Grass, now the desired feed of the punished.
Loneliness consumes my dark places.
My God, I bow.

Lost years of disgrace forgiven,
I seek to honor thee.
New beginnings humble my soul;
I, but a servant, serve thee.

Reflection

I connected with an old friend on Facebook after more than 25 years. In our reminiscing, we talked about many of our childhood follies. But one memory in particular stood out—our time playing sand lot football. Imagine, if you will, my being, not just the biggest kid, but "Big Doug." When the team needed five yards, they gave it to "Big Doug." When they needed to stop someone, they pointed "Big Doug" in that direction. Yet, I had a weakness, and the kids I hung around with were the only ones who knew it.

When we played against one another, they knew what to do get me to forget the rules by jumping offside, holding or causing some other penalty, they would just irritate me so much that I would get angry. Then they would get the biggest laugh at my expense. I was Big Doug, the "king of the field," except I did not have a field to call my own.

Through much of my adult life, I was unable to control my emotions, allowing people to push my buttons. I am not saying that I have control of my emotions yet. But, what I do have is a Father in heaven who is working with me to fix this defect of my character. As the Bible says: "Pride leads to disgrace, but with humility comes wisdom" (Prov. 11:2, NLT). For me, incarceration provided an opportunity for humility. Accepting responsibility for the mistakes I have made, shows growth in my character. Look out wisdom, here I come!

Thought

In today's world, the individual reigns supreme, meaning there is great freedom for self-expression. The idea that this is something new, however, is ridiculous. Visual artist Andy Warhol, architect Frank Lloyd Wright, and others epitomized success without undue pride. Pride destroys, so why not enjoy success without the exclamation points?

Prayer

God, I traveled this path once before, and I failed. If You would bless me to travel this path once more, this time, I will let you lead.

Scripture

"Now I, Nebuchadnezzar, praise and extol and honor the King of heaven, all of whose works are truth, and His ways justice. And those who walk in pride He is able to put down." (Dan. 4:37, NKJV)

Group/Individual Study

A. Begin with prayer.
B. Read the scripture aloud.
C. Reflect on the scripture.
D. Answer the thought questions.

Thought Questions

1. Humility became my hiding place. If Jesus humbled Himself to love everyone He met, why do hurt and anger hide behind humility?

2. Are pride and anger, which cause division, weapons of God?

3. If pride goes before the fall, why then do so many knowingly choose the fall?

4. Aggressive power hungry people often push others' buttons to take opportunistic advantage of them. Who likes taking advantage of such a situation? Does this describe you or someone you know?

Day 26.

MY STEPS

I rise, for blessing engulf this space;
For I am, and we are one.
Our travels from midnight through dawn,
My steps ordained by Father and Son.

Images of blue hues seem endless,
Like the sea, the waters, blues and greens.
And yet, as I look out, I feel the passion of the sea,
A depth of compassion, Your reign over me.

Shades of gray follow my life, as drops of rain fall in spring,
Soaking up worldly greed as a sponge, I exceed my bounds.
Engulfed in darkness, the light of peace sought to reclaim me.
A love, a depth of character, Lord, my passion to serve thee.

A calling not known, not known to me, I search for my place.
When death knocked, the shots fired—fired toward my face.
Falling to my knees, my tears engulfed me.
Like the blue-green face of the sea,
I see the calling God laid gently, and particularly, for me.

Reflection

This poem has a special place in my heart, for, on a pleasant October morning, six shots rang out at me close range. An angel must have been with me that morning, because not a single bullet hit me. One round hit my car, leaving a hole in the hood. Where the other five rounds went, only God knows. So, when I wrote this poem and every time I read it again, tears fill my eyes.

I fooled myself for a while into thinking that I was just in the wrong place at the wrong time. However, the truth is that gray was the color of my life at that time, and I was there doing what I had planned. Yet, I had not figured on the alternate plan the enemy had for me. The sea is so vast that no one notices a pebble going into the water unless they see it going in. I thank God that He was watching me.

The tears I have cried are as vast as the sea. Unlike the silent pebble, many have seen my tears. God put them there to hold, support, and guide me back to the shore because He has a purpose particularly for me.

Thought

The love of family cannot be underestimated. However, family is not and cannot be always where we need them. Though it may sound cliché, God is everywhere, an ever-present help when we need Him (Psalm 46:1). To understand how this can be, one must have faith in God.

Prayer

My God, there are many who ask how I can talk to emptiness. I pray that these be given a glimpse of the glory of Your kingdom that they might believe.

Scripture

"The steps of a good man are ordered by the LORD, and He delights in his way. Though he fall, he shall not be utterly cast down; for the LORD upholds him with His hand." (Psalm 37:23, 24, NKJV)

Group/Individual Study

A. Begin with prayer.
B. Read the scripture aloud.
C. Reflect on the scripture.
D. Answer the thought questions.

Thought Questions

1. Have you ever witnessed an accident and thought it could have been you? Did you superficially give God thanks, or did you praise Him from your heart?

2. Do you really believe that God doesn't make mistakes?

3. The author believes God ordains his steps. How do you see your calling? Do you believe that you have a calling of any kind?

4. Looking at the vast openness of the ocean and the sky, can God really be everywhere and be with all the people who inhabit the earth?

Day 27.

DARK PATHS

Treacherous byways, concrete highways,
Black tar, the shimmer of heat rises.
Trouble surrounds me like a salted sea.
A hairless man, skull bald, a head of sweat beads.

Waves of heat, glistening from the black tar
My feet burn, the image of hell, I stand.
Cool ice relieves as the promised word.
A journey of life and death, cursed, I endure.

Sweat travels across the brows
Eyes burn, I stand too close to the fire.
Sweet taste of salt plunders the palate.
Shades of darkness, the slow drip of life.

My flesh seeks the pleasures of life.
Like the Dead Sea, I will perish.
Lord, Your Word is life, and this life is death.
Not forsaking the promise, I seek Your gift of life.

Dark Paths

Cross the byways, cross the concrete,
Enduring sweat, the sting of water running free.
Renewed strength parting the crazy life I lead.
Truth gleaned through darkness carries me free.

Reflection

Imagine that it is pouring down freezing rain, yet your addiction is calling. So, you dress up in five layers of clothes and set out walking. If this walk were just around the corner, it would be no big thing. But it isn't. It is five miles out and back. It may seem ludicrous for me to do this instead of staying home where it was warm. Yet, when the lion roars, someone somewhere will answer. That night it was me.

I walked ten miles in freezing temperatures (which isn't so much when you consider that thousands run under the same conditions for exercise and think nothing of it). What pulled me away from my warm, dry house was my addiction. Addictions are distractions. When Peter got out of the boat at Jesus' command, he was walking on water until he became distracted. Ever since Satan was kicked out of heaven to the earth, addictions have been the devil's playground. That is why it is important to keep our eyes on Jesus, the prize.

Jesus said, "I am the way, the truth, and the life. No one comes to the Father except through me" (John 14:6, NKJV). Give Caesar what belongs to Caesar, but, Satan, keep your drugs, alcohol, and other stuff. I'll keep Jesus.

Thought

Imagine your worst nightmare. Now picture yourself fully engaged in it, though it is not a dream, for you are living it every day. The worst thing about it is that you are not living it by force but by choice. Many people live this way without knowing how or wanting to turn on the light. Yet, they too are God's children, and we must continue to pray for them.

Prayer

Lord, I thank You for always being with me—even when I did not desire Your presence. I thank You for proving the word true—You would never leave me or forsake me.

Scripture
"Be sober, be vigilant; because your adversary the devil, as a roaring lion, walketh about, seeking whom he may devour." (1 Peter 5:8, NKJ)

Group/Individual Study

A. Begin with prayer.
B. Read the scripture aloud.
C. Reflect on the scripture.
D. Answer the thought questions.

Thought Questions

1. Peter walked on water to get to Jesus, his prize. Where are you willing to walk to get to your prize?

2. The lion's roar represents sin's "call." We all have fallen short of God's glory (Rom. 3:23). Think about the last time that you answered the lion's roar.

3. If the things that we collect on earth belong to the earth, why do we strive so hard to hold onto them, knowing that they cannot go with us to heaven?

4. The poem reads like a trip to purgatory. Does it describe a place you would like to visit?

Day 28.

DECEIVED

Guilt drives strong thoughts of desire.
Shock and disbelief reverberates when deceived.
Stones heaved into that mirror of trust,
A soul drained of conviction gathers disbelief.

Hiding compassion in dark places of the mind,
Betrayal is life, and truth is so easily broken.
Damaged candor, fractured heart,
A soul in need of mending, in need of peace.

Darkness covers the eyes and sin fills the soul.
Wandering thoughts loosed not bound, seek relief.
Father, Your conviction is great and Your mercy pleasing.
Lord, how do I trust, when those I trust are full of deceit?

Into the light, the Son will shine, for He is the way.
From bent knees sense the reign of Him
Who loves you from on high.
Exposed we fall; unhurried, Lord, we fall upon our knees.

Knowing beyond the sanctuary doors he lies.
The weapon, sin, drives deep it cuts and remains within.
Satan, you deceived; the Lord is my comforter,
Whose face and tender mercy's judgment I seek.

Reflection

I could feel sorry for myself for the many opportunities I once had and lost because of my impatience and dogged and brash independence, coupled with the need to prove my worth. Oh, I certainly had "credentials," but they are now past tense. Now, with a criminal history, finding employment is the highest mountain I ever had to climb.

Society talks a good game of second chances, but apparently everyone hasn't gotten the memo. I believe that most people go to church for the sake of appearance, forgetting that Jesus died for their real second chance. I have fallen, but I refuse to stay down. Let me say something to the young people—and especially the black males—in America: Second chances don't come freely. My best advice is: Choose not to need one.

I believed in the system but discovered a lie that redefined America for me. Fortunately, America is made up of people, and not all people wear masks. Some are real, and their second chances are real too. I thank these people for the real second chances they have given.

Thought

A word to the Fast-talking people out to make a buck: Do you think God's kingdom awaits you? Deception is not the mark of God. If that is how you earn your living, you need to consider a new line of work!

Prayer

For many years I have said, Lord, I never want to achieve success by stepping upon another. I thank You, Father, for the ability and desire to learn and honestly earn my way through life.

Scripture
"And while He was still speaking, behold, a multitude; and he who was called Judas, one of the twelve, went before them and drew near to Jesus to kiss Him. But Jesus said to him, 'Judas, are you betraying the Son of Man with a kiss?' " (Luke 22:47, 48, NKJV)

Group/Individual Study
A. Begin with prayer.
B. Read the scripture aloud.
C. Reflect on the scripture.
D. Answer the thought questions.

Thought Questions

1. Has the American educational system prepared children who graduate from high school to be productive, responsible, and participating adults in society?
   A. Is the educational system totally to blame?
   B. What responsibility rests upon parents?

2. Second chances are nice, but should everyone be given one?

3. Is it the responsibility of the business sector to be the moral barometer of a society and offer second chances? Or are second chances the business of the church?

4. Is trust as fragile as a mirror?

5. Why are we unhurried to fall to our knees when we go to God?

Day 29.

DARKNESS TO REDEMPTION

Harboring darkness, death's place in the mind,
Dark lonely experience, real place, void of time.
Soft sweet swirls of smoke, a still soft breeze,
Ambiguous sites and visions both day and night.

Shiftless acquisitions quicken time.
Confinement of the mind, my mind,
Doing time again and again.
A vagabond drifting, acquiring property away,
Replicates the same story day after day.

Dark, lonely experiences, spirits and visions,
A desperate plea for freedom, sightless hostile division.
The favor of God, faith in Christ, its manifestation
The Trinity is, thus we have favor.

Righteousness knows; the conscience believes.
The soul is relieved as darkness flees.
Seize life's covering; follow the light within;
Rebuke all darkness; discover the solace from sin.

Reflection

There was a time when I wanted to run away. I felt so much pressure from the world around me. This was during my pre-teen years, when my inferiority complex was running rampant. Escape—any escape—was what I sought, whether through a dream or an altered state. I knew the church, its name, and where it stood, but that is all. No one ever taught me about its meaning, and I did not ask.

Over the years, I sought to find my identity through people and things. In my marriage and work, the failures mounted. In individual endeavors, I would find success. However, in social settings, no matter how I tried, I just did not fit in. It became easy to slide into the darkness of despair that for so long became my home.

Smiling outwardly, while crying for help within, I did not know where to turn or who to confide in. Society's two faces disappointed me. I had to crash and burn to find hope. God showed His mercy as the Disciples of Christ Ministry saved my life.

Thought

Educational choices were limited to many African American students in earlier American history. However, those who chose not to remain in the dark did not take "no" for an answer but seized, and sometimes made, opportunities when they came available. Thus, their determination won out over quitting and over blaming others for their circumstances. We are what we choose to make ourselves.

Prayer

Lord, You made us in Your image and yet we choose to think like humans. Bless me with wisdom so that I may gain the knowledge to understand Your ways.

Scripture
"For by me your days will be multiplied, and years of life will be added to you. If you are wise, you are wise for yourself, and if you scoff, you alone will bear it." (Prov. 9:11, 12, NKJV)

Group/Individual Study

A. Begin with prayer.
B. Read the scripture aloud.
C. Reflect on the scripture.
D. Answer the thought questions.

Thought Questions

1. Have you ever felt trapped by your own thinking? Share the thought with your group or write it down and explore your feelings.

2. Christ told His disciples that faith the size of a mustard seed could move a mountain. Jesus was speaking figuratively, but is faith powerful enough to literally change you?

3. In discovering solace through my devotion to Christ Jesus, I found something more—fellowship. Is this, perhaps, the Father's intent?

4. Parents, are you teaching your children what church is really about, or are you sending them to church and hoping they will come to understand on their own?

5. When you need help, which friend do you call—the one whose number is on speed dial or the one for whom all you have to do is cry out the name "Jesus"?

Day 30.

A SINNER'S PRAYER

In my mind I stood alone.
A whore on streets of violence.
Evil besieged me, a family affair.
I now know, Lord, that You were there.

Brothers and cousins work their wares.
Gang members stand together here.
Only the whore comes here alone,
Praying, please forgive me, Lord, once more.

I read Your truth, though not every day.
I even know and sometimes pray.
I truly want You to change my life.
My capacity for loving blocks my love of Christ.

Teach me the promises of Your guiding truth.
Let words from my mouth reverence You.
Allow the will of the Father's love
To save this child from Satan's claws.

Though my actions are sick, my heart is good.
Allow me, Father, to rest in Your word.
A sinner I am, oh Lord, just a man.
My God, my God, grant me another chance.

Reflection
If you are outnumbered four to one, is it worth the fight? When the lion roars, you are reacting and not thinking. That is why I believe so many addicts find themselves in situations of their own making. Fortunately, the day of my dangerous situation, angels watched over me.

I truly believe that I only survived my experience because God was with me. I carried His presence everywhere, even though I was doing wrong. We often hear people say, "God knows my heart." I believe many people use that thought as an excuse to do wrong. I was a lost, confused soul, yet I still knew God. Though I was living a sinful life, there was a line that knowledge of God kept me from crossing.

The following prayer of repentance is for anyone who is willing to say, "Lord, here I am. Please forgive me." Jesus died to give us all the opportunity to go to the Father and ask for forgiveness. The real question is: Does He know you? Have you given Christ your life? If not, find a church home and do so today. *Tomorrow is not guaranteed.*

Thought
It is a wonderful feeling to know that we are never alone, no matter what. Whether we are right or wrong, the Father is there. Just like God's first children in Eden, we choose to hide our face when we do wrong. Yet, our God sees and waits for us to come home again.

Prayer
Lord, You know where I am mentally and physically as I write. I ask You to forgive me. Forgive me, Father, for I have hurt so many, but, worst of all, I sinned against You. Please forgive me.

Scripture

"And the tax collector, standing afar off, would not so much as raise his eyes to heaven, but beat his breast, saying, 'God be merciful to me a sinner!' "I tell you, this man went down to his house justified rather than the other; for everyone one who exalts himself will be abased, and he who humbles himself will be exalted.' " (Luke 18:13, 14, NKJV)

Group/Individual Study

A. Begin with prayer.
B. Read the scripture aloud.
C. Reflect on the scripture.
D. Answer the thought questions.

Thought Questions

1. In this poem, I said I stood alone only because that is what I believed at the time. Does God really leave us even when we're doing wrong?

2. The Bible describes going to the Father and asking for forgiveness. Will God forgive you infinitely?

3. Though God does know the human heart, does that give us an excuse not to have a relationship with Him or a knowledge of the Bible?

4. We were all born into sin. We matriculated in sin and have advanced degrees in it. Do we have a responsibility to help one another when tempted?

5. If we are evangelizing as Jesus calls us to do, does it matter with whom we share?
    a. Does it matter where we share?
    b. Can an addict become an evangelist?

In loving memory of Mrs. Shirley A. Boyer-Davis.

Mother of four, Douglas, Donna, Sheila, and Sheldon.

We miss you but know you're in a better place.

TEACH Services, Inc.
P U B L I S H I N G

We invite you to view the complete
selection of titles we publish at:
www.TEACHServices.com

We encourage you to write us
with your thoughts about this,
or any other book we publish at:
info@TEACHServices.com

TEACH Services' titles may be purchased in
bulk quantities for educational, fund-raising,
business, or promotional use.
bulksales@TEACHServices.com

Finally, if you are interested in seeing
your own book in print, please contact us at:
publishing@TEACHServices.com

We are happy to review your manuscript at no charge.

www.ingramcontent.com/pod-product-compliance
Lightning Source LLC
Chambersburg PA
CBHW050821160426
43192CB00010B/1847